SMA

Music compiled by Peter Evans and Peter Lavender
Song background notes by Michael Kennedy

All text photographs courtesy of Hulton Getty
except MSI (Pages 3, 4, 5, 8, 11 & 12)

Cover photograph of Marilyn Monroe
from The Kobal Collection

Edited by Pearce Marchbank

Text researched and compiled by Heather Page
Book design by Pearce Marchbank and Ben May
Picture research by Nicki Russell

Printed in the United Kingdom by
Page Bros Ltd, Norwich, Norfolk

Exclusive Distributors:
Music Sales Limited
89 Frith Street,
London W1V 5TZ, England.
Music Sales Pty Limited
120 Rothschild Avenue,
Rosebery, NSW 2018,
Australia.

Order No. AM92358
ISBN 0-7119-4434-2
This book © Copyright 1997
Wise Publications

Your Guarantee of Quality
As publishers, we strive to produce every book
to the highest commercial standards.
This book has been carefully designed to minimise
awkward page turns and to make playing from
it a real pleasure.
Particular care has been given to specifying acid-free,
neutral-sized paper made from pulps which have not
been elemental chlorine bleached. This pulp is from
farmed sustainable forests and was produced with
special regard for the environment.
Throughout, the printing and binding have been
planned to ensure a sturdy, attractive publication
which should give years of enjoyment.
If your copy fails to meet our high standards,
please inform us and we will gladly replace it.

Music Sales' complete catalogue describes thousands
of titles and is available in full colour sections by
subject, direct from Music Sales Limited.
Please state your areas of interest and send a
cheque/postal order for £1.50 for postage to:
Music Sales Limited, Newmarket Road, Bury St.
Edmunds, Suffolk IP33 3YB.

Visit the Internet Music Shop at
http://www.musicsales.co.uk

Wise Publications
London/New York/Paris/Sydney/Copenhagen/Madrid

9.95

The records seem to be changed about once a fortnight by the hiring firm; almost all are American; almost all are 'vocals' and the styles of singing much advanced beyond what is normally heard on the Light Programme of the BBC … The 'nickelodeon' is allowed to blare out so that the noise would be sufficient to fill a good-sized ballroom, rather than a converted shop in the main street. The young men waggle one shoulder or stare, as desperately as Humphrey Bogart, across the tubular chairs.
RICHARD HOGGART ON MILK BARS
IN HIS BOOK 'THE USES OF LITERACY'

Two out of three families in the country now own television, one in three has a car or motor cycle, twice as many are taking holidays away from home - these are welcome signs of the increasing enjoyment of leisure …
CONSERVATIVE PARTY ELECTION
MANIFESTO, 1959

The whole town mourns the loss as do thousands upo thousands of other peopl Everyone is deeply shocke
COUNCILLOR EDWARD REID ON T
PLANE CRASH THAT KILLED SEV
MANCHESTER UNITED PLAYERS AN
THREE OFFICIALS, 19

The story is of course utterly untrue. It is quite unthinkable that a royal princess, third in line of succession to the throne, should even contemplate a marriage with a man who has been through the divorce courts.

'THE PEOPLE' ON PRINCESS MARGARET'S RELATIONSHIP WITH PETER TOWNSEND

The return of the Queen to Londo should be as quiet as possible… it is accordingly hoped that there v be no public gathering at London airport tomorrow afternoon.

DOWNING STREET ANNOUNCEMENT ON THE DEATH OF GEORGE VI, 1952

The heart of the comrade and inspired continuer of Lenin's will, the wise leader and teacher of the Communist party and the Soviet people, Joseph Vissarionovitch Stalin, has stopped beating.

MOSCOW RADIO ANNOUNCEMENT, MARCH 1953

I have reached this decision entire alone… I am deeply grateful for th concern of all those who ha constantly prayed for my happine:

PRINCESS MARGARET, ANNOUNCING TH SHE WILL NOT MARRY GROUP CAPTA PETER TOWNSEND, 19

We have been laughing at their gay
little madnesses, my dear, at their
point-to-points, at the postural
slumps of the well-off and mentally
under-privileged, at their stooping
shoulders and strained accents, at
their waffling cant for too long.
JOHN OSBORNE ON THE
BRITISH RULING CLASS

Showery but with sunny
intervals; during the afternoon,
some showers will be heavy,
with hail and thunder.
WEATHER FORECAST ON
CORONATION DAY, JUNE 1953

Everest has been conquered by the
British expedition. The climbers to
reach the summit of the 29,002ft
peak were E P Hillary, the New
Zealander, and Tensing, the Sherpa.
REPORT IN 'THE DAILY TELEGRAPH',
CORONATION DAY, JUNE 1953

Man entered the Space Age
yesterday when Russia rocketed
an earth satellite - a man-made
'moon' - into outer space. It is
now circling the world 560 miles
up once every 95 minutes.
'DAILY EXPRESS', OCTOBER 1957,
ON THE LAUNCH OF THE FIRST SPUTNIK

Terribly sorry for my silence.
Am embarking on a long
Mediterranean holiday.
Do forgive. Guy.
A TELEGRAM FROM GUY BURGESS,
WHO 'DISAPPEARED' IN MAY 1951,
TO HIS MOTHER

A tuppenny Punch and Judy show.
SIR WINSTON CHURCHILL ON THE
NEW COMMERCIAL TELEVISION, 1955

He is Pan, he is Puck, h
every nice young girl's b
every kid's favourite el
brother, every mothe
cherished adolescent s
COLIN MACINNES ON TOMMY STE
BRITAIN'S FIRST ROCK 'N' ROLL S

I think it is degrading. The boys look silly. Some have tried it on, but I have told them that if they wear their hair in that way they would have to go elsewhere.

NORTH LONDON HEADMASTER
ON THE 'EDWARDIAN' HAIR STYLES
ADOPTED BY HIS SCHOOLBOYS

Some of our people have never had it so good.

HAROLD MACMILLAN

We all enjoyed the first performance. Rowdies and troublemakers turned up for the next show and we had to call in the police.

GAUMONT CINEMA MANAGER,
DAGENHAM, ON TEDDY BOYS
AND GIRLS DANCING IN THE
AISLES DURING THE FILM 'ROCK
AROUND THE CLOCK', 1956

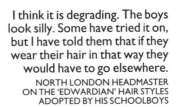

"I'm all right Jack" became a way of life, a national anthem. It was a Tory decade.

'NEW STATESMAN' ON THE
1950'S IN JANUARY, 1960

The number of British films that have ever made a genuine try at a story in a popular milieu, with working-class characters all through, can be counted on the fingers of one hand.

LINDSAY ANDERSON,
FILM DIRECTOR

us welcome to our shores
many members of our
ish Commonwealth, and
the visitors from other
ds who have come to see
at this old country can do.

RGE VI OPENING THE
TIVAL OF BRITAIN, 1951

The first four-minute mi
the history of athletics
accomplished here toda
Roger Gilbert Bannis
25 year-old medical stud
who was timed offic
to run the distanc
3 minutes 59.4 seco
'DAILY TELEGRAPH', MAY

What the hero's predicament was,
apart from the hint that he was
"born out of his time", I found
difficult to decide. He was, perhaps,
a character who should have gone
to a psychiatrist rather than have
come to a dramatist - not at any
rate to one writing his first play.
CRITIC PATRICK GIBBS ON JIMMY PORTER,
HERO OF JOHN OSBORNE'S
'LOOK BACK IN ANGER', 1956

I'm just one of the millions, the fans, the
expectant, sobbing, screaming mass…
You'd flash us that special, pouty grin,
swivelling those hips in our direction…
ELVIS PRESLEY FAN, 1957

This annual ritual attracted
derision of the press, wh
concentrated its ridicule on
outstanding eccentric, the bear
and tousled non-conformists v
the guitars, ignoring the long
patient tramping columns of wh
normal and unremarka
housewives and workers
shopkeepers and clerk
JAMES CAMERON ON THE ANNUAL (
ALDERMASTON MARCH, STARTED IN
(SEE FOLLOWING PA

Memories Are Made Of This

Words & Music by Terry Gilkyson, Richard Dehr & Frank Miller.

Although 'Memories Are Made Of This' was featured in a Mario Lanza film, The Seven Hills Of Rome, the hit recording of this catchy Terry Gilkyson, Richard Dehr and Frank Miller song was made by Mr Relaxation himself, Dean Martin, who enjoyed four weeks at No. 1 in Britain and a further five at the same position in America.

Take one fresh and ten-der kiss___

Add one sto-len night of bliss___ One girl

one boy Some grief some joy Mem - o - ries are made of this.

Don't for - get a small moon - beam__
With some bless-ings from a - bove__

Fold in light- ly with a dream.
Serve it gen-'rous-ly with love.__

Your lips and mine, Two sips of wine, Mem - or -
One man, one wife, One love thro' life, Mem - or -

To Coda

ies are made of this.__ Then add the
ies are made of this.__

wed-ding bells, One house where lov-ers dwell, Three lit-tle kids___ For the fla-vour, _____ Stir care-f'lly thro' the days See how the fla-vour stays. These are the dreams you will sav - our.

D.%. al Coda

CODA

Mem - or - ies are made of this._____

15

C'Est Si Bon

Music by Henri Betti. Original Lyrics by André Hornez.
English Lyrics by Jerry Seelen.

A piquant up-tempo delight, 'C'est Si Bon' will always be associated with Eartha Kitt, who sang it in New Faces. It was also a hit for country and western star Conway Twitty. The song, a hit in the London show Latin Quarter, is French, and was written by Henri Betti and André Hornez, with an English lyric by Jerry Seelen.

16

17

18

Your Cheatin' Heart

Words & Music by Hank Williams.

Alabama-born country star and distinguished songwriter Hank Williams was only 30 when he died of a heart attack on the way to an engagement in Ohio. His legacy is a treasure trove of fine songs and recordings. 'Your Cheatin' Heart', also the title of a film biography, is one of the best of these. The song was also memorably recorded by Connie Francis and Patsy Cline.

come _____ the whole night through. _____
come _____ when you'll be blue. _____

Your cheat-in' _____ heart _____ will tell on you. _____

— When tears come down _____ like fall - in'

rain, _____ you'll toss a - round _____

20

Cry

Words & Music by Churchill Kohlman.

Johnnie Ray was perhaps the only great rock star to wear a hearing aid. He specialised in weepy ballads, choosing as his signature tune Churchill Kohlman's 'Cry' which topped the American charts for eleven weeks. Such was Ray's involvement with his songs that he managed to cry real tears each time he sang.

If your sweet-heart sends a let-ter of good-bye, It's no se-cret you'll feel bet-ter if you cry When wak-ing from a bad dream don't you some-times think it's real? But it's on-ly false e-mo-tions that you

The Song From Moulin Rouge
(Where Is Your Heart)

Words by William Engvick. Music by Georges Auric.

French classical composer Georges Auric penned a beautiful melody for Jane Avril (Zsa Zsa Gabor) to sing in Moulin Rouge, John Huston's evocative, beautiful film celebration of the life and art of Henri de Toulouse-Lautrec. Based on a novel by Pierre LaMure, the film starred José Ferrer as the painter. The song was 'Where Is Your Heart?', with words by William Engvick

this, I wor - ry and won - der, You're close to me here, but where is your heart? It's a sad thing to re - al - ize that you've a heart that nev - er melts. When we kiss, do you close your

eyes, pre - tend-ing that I'm some - one else? You must break the spell, this cloud that I'm un - der. So please won't you tell, dar - ling, where is your heart? When - heart?

dim. e rall.

From Here To Eternity

Words by Robert Wells. Music by Fred Karger.

1953 saw the release of a tough no-holds barred war film From Here To Eternity which featured that passionate seaweed-encrusted kiss for Burt Lancaster and Deborah Kerr. Fine performances too from sensitive Montgomery Clift, and from Frank Sinatra, who subsequently recorded the title music as a song, written by Bob Wells and Fred Karger.

Moderately, with expression

CHORUS

You vowed your love, from here to e-ter-ni-ty, a love so true, it nev-er would die. You

gave your lips, _____ gave them so will - ing - ly, _____

_____ how could I know _____ your kiss meant good -

bye? _____ Now I'm a - lone,

_____ with on - ly a me - mo - ry, _____ my

emp - ty arms _____ will nev - er know why. _____

'Tho' you are gone, _____ this love that you

left with me, _____ will live from here to e -

ter - ni - ty. _____

Here's That Rainy Day

Words & Music by Johnny Burke & Jimmy Van Heusen.

Just because the show's a flop, that's no reason for its songs to fail. 'Here's That Rainy Day' was introduced by the radiant Dolores Gray, star of London's Annie Get Your Gun and Follies, in the little remembered Broadway show Carnival In Flanders. The writers were Johnny Burke and Jimmy Van Heusen. There are fine recordings by Frank Sinatra, Peggy Lee and Tony Bennett.

Slowly, with expression

May-be I should have saved those left-ov-er dreams; fun-ny, but here's that rain-y day.

Here's that rain-y day they

Fun - ny how love be - comes a cold rain - y day. Fun - ny that rain - y day is here.

1.

2.

here.

rall.

Shake, Rattle And Roll

Words & Music by Charles Calhoun.

'The father of Rock 'n' Roll' was the somewhat inaccurate title used in Bill Haley's publicity. Yet this middle-aged rocker enjoyed a massive hit with Joe Turner's 1954 rhythm and blues success 'Shake, Rattle And Roll', written by Charles Calhoun. Haley's version reached No.4 in 1955 in Britain, following seventh position in America the previous year.

Moderately Bright

VERSE

Get out ___ from that kitch-en and rat-tle those pots and pans, ___

Get out ___ from that kitch-en and rat-tle those pots and pans. ___

Well, roll my break-fast, 'cause_ I'm a hun-gry man. ___

CHORUS

Shake Rat-tle and Roll, ___ Shake rat-tle and roll,

Shake rat-tle and roll, ___ Shake rat-tle and roll;

You nev-er do noth-in' to save your dog-gone

I Left My Heart In San Francisco

Words by Douglas Cross. Music by George Cory.

Anthony Dominick Benedetto is a fine painter, but also one of the finest popular singers of the 20th century - as Tony Bennett. Bennett was born in the Queens borough of New York in 1926, but in the words of his theme song, written by Douglas Cross and George Cory, 'I Left My Heart in San Francisco.' Originally written in 1954, the song won an American Grammy in 1962.

Everyone's forgotten the prison drama Unchained but its hit song lives on. A hit first of all for Al Hibbler, for Jimmy Young, for the Righteous Brothers in the 60s and the 80s and recently for those two stars of Soldier, Soldier Robson Green and Jerome Flynn, who took it to the top of the charts in the mid 1990s. Hy Zaret and Alex North wrote the song.

Unchained Melody

Music by Alex North. Words by Hy Zaret.

Moderately slow

Oh, my love, my dar-ling, I've hun-gered for your touch a long, lone-ly time. _____ Time goes by so slow-ly and time can do so much, Are you still

mine? _____ I need your love, _____ I need your love, _____

God speed your love _____ to me! _____

A little faster
1. Lone - ly riv - ers flow _____ to the sea, _____ to the sea,
2. Lone - ly moun - tains gaze _____ at the stars, _____ at the stars,

poco accel.

To the o - pen arms _____ of the sea. _____
Wait - ing for the dawn _____ of the day. _____

43

44

Love Me Tender

Words & Music by Elvis Presley & Vera Matson.

'Love Me Tender' was based on a popular ballad of 1861, 'Aura Lee', and was thus ideal for the period Western Love Me Tender that was the film début of Elvis Presley in 1956. Presley wrote 'Love Me Tender' with Vera Matson. It was a tender ballad, worlds away from rock 'n' roll, and spent five weeks at No. 1 in America, reaching 11th place in Britain.

Moderately slow

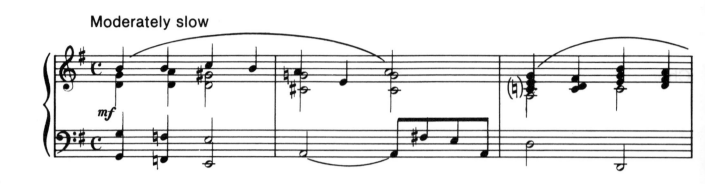

Verse

1. Love Me Ten - der, love me sweet;
2. Love Me Ten - der, love me long;
3. Love Me Ten - der, love me dear;

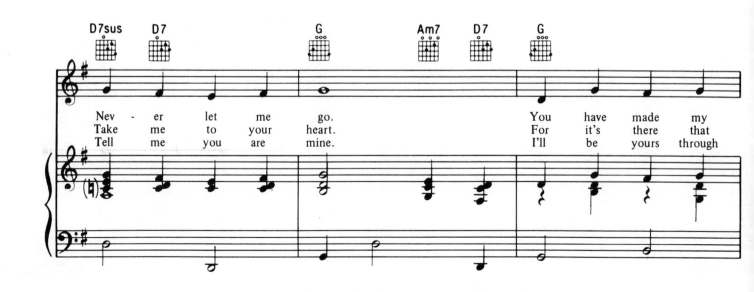

Nev - er let me go. You have made my
Take me to your heart. For it's made there that
Tell me you are mine. I'll be yours through

46

EXTRA VERSE   4. When at last my dreams come true,
                 Darling, this I know:
                 Happiness will follow you
                 Everywhere you go.

Tennessee-born Carl Perkins was a country and rockabilly singer and composer. He took his own composition 'Blue Suede Shoes' into the American charts. In Britain the song had the distinction of being Elvis Presley's first Top Ten hit, reaching No.9 in mid 1956. Presley's version was not a comparable hit in the States, however, where the composer's version reigned supreme.

Blue Suede Shoes

Words & Music by Carl Lee Perkins.

49

Witchcraft

Words by Carolyn Leigh. Music by Cy Coleman.

© Copyright 1957 (renewed 1985) Morley Music Company, USA.
Campbell Connelly & Company Limited, 8/9 Frith Street, London W1V 5TZ (50%)/
EMI Songs Limited, 127 Charing Cross Road, London WC2 (50%).
All Rights Reserved. International Copyright Secured.

When you a - rouse the need in me, my heart says,
"Yes, in - deed" in me, "Pro - ceed with what you're lead - in' me to!"
It's such an an - cient pitch But one I would - n't switch
'Cause there's no nic - er witch than you!
you!

Good Golly Miss Molly

Words & Music by Robert Blackwell & John Marascalco.

Although Little Richard (Penniman) enjoyed a massive American hit with 'Good Golly Miss Molly', it was the British pop group The Swingin' Blue Jeans who took Robert Blackwell and John Marascalco's perennial rock 'n' roll smash to No.11 in our charts – they even managed 43rd place in the States. Good for them!

Mom-ma, Pop-pa told me "Son you'd bet-ter watch your step" What I knew a-bout Miss Mol-ly, Got-ta

watch my dad-dy my-self. Good Gol - ly Miss Mol - ly

Yeah you sure _ like a ball _____ When you're shak - in' and a

shout - in'   Can't you hear_your Mom-ma   call?

Peggy Sue

Words & Music by Jerry Allison, Norman Petty & Buddy Holly.

'Peggy Sue' was written by Buddy Holly, Jerry Allison of the Crickets backing group, and their manager Norman Petty. The subject was the girlfriend of a member of the group. The song was Holly's only US Top Ten chart entry, reaching No.3. In Britain it was merely the first, reaching No.6. It is featured in the long running British show Buddy. The song was originally called 'Cindy Lou!'

Peg - gy Sue;_____ Oh, well, I

love you gal,_____ and I need you, Peg - gy Sue._____

I love you,_____

Peg - gy Sue,_____ With a love so rare and true,_

58

That'll Be The Day

Words & Music by Norman Petty, Buddy Holly & Jerry Allison.

The title of a fine British pop film starring David Essex, 'That'll Be The Day' was written by the creative triumvirate Buddy Holly, Norman Petty and Jerry Allison. It did not reach the Top Ten in 1957, but rapidly became a classic. Holly, born Charles Holley, hailed from Lubbock, Texas, His premature death in an air crash was a severe blow to popular music.

Moderately, with a beat

Verse 1

Well, you give me all your lov-in' and your tur-tle-dov-in', All — your hugs an' kiss-es an' your mon-ey too; — Well, you know you love me, ba-by, Un-til you tell me, may-be, that some day, well, I'll be through! Well, —

Chorus

Diana

Words & Music by Paul Anka.

Canadian singer/composer Paul Anka was barely sixteen years old when his recording of the self-penned song 'Diana' stormed the world's pop charts, selling over nine million records. It was the story of his love for a girl four years older than himself. This, and other songs by Anka dealing with teenage love and frustration, found an answering chord in his legion of fans.

Medium Rock

I'm so young and you're so old. This my dar-ling I've been told. I don't care just what they say 'cause for-ev-er I will pray you and I will be as free as the birds up in the trees. Oh please stay by

All I Have To Do Is Dream

Words & Music by Boudleaux Bryant.

Seven weeks at the top of the British charts - that was the reward for Boudleaux Bryant, for a song that it is said took only fifteen minutes to write. The singers were the Everly Brothers, and the year, 1958. It was their biggest seller and remained at the top of the American charts for four weeks. In 1970 Glenn Campbell and Bobbie Gentry brought the song back to No.3.

need you so that I could die, I love you so

and that is why When-ev-er I want you — all I have to do is

1. dream. _____ **2.** dream, _____

dream, dream, dream. — Dream, _____ dream, dream, dream, — dream.

rit.

Fever

Words & Music by John Davenport & Eddie Cooley.

It seems as if John Davenport and Eddie Cooley will be remembered for just one song - but what a song! 'Fever', forever associated with the cool, hip recording by Peggy Lee, is one of the most evocative songs of the Fifties. It was also featured by Keely Smith and Louis Prima in their musical picture Hey Boy! Hey Girl!

1. Nev-er know how much I love you, nev-er know how much I care. When you put your arms a-round me, I get a fev-er that's so hard to bear.

2. Sun lights up the day-time, moon lights up the night. I light up when you call my name, and you know I'm gon-na treat you right. You give me fev-er

when you kiss me, fev - er when you hold⸻ me tight.

Fev - er in the morn - ing, fev - er all through⸻ the night.

night. Ev - 'ry - bo - dy's

got the fev - er, that is some - thing

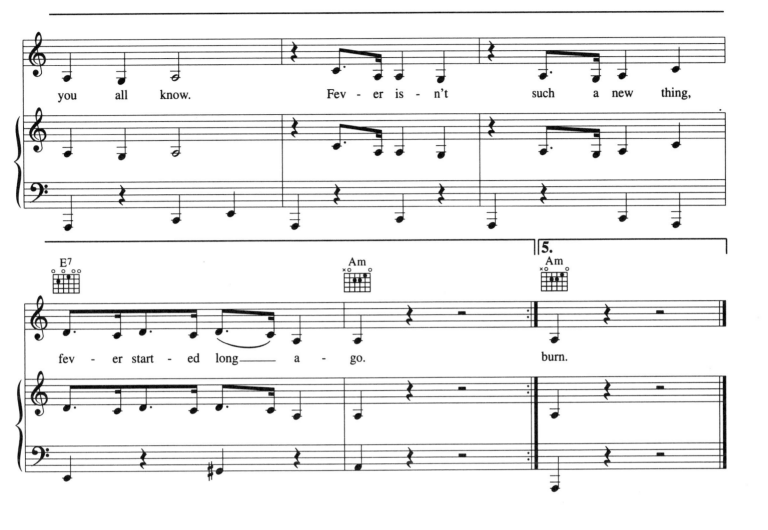

Verse 3:
Romeo loved Juliet,
Juliet she felt the same,
When he put his arms around her, he said
"Julie, baby you're my flame."

CHORUS:
Thou givest fever, when we kisseth
Fever with thy flaming youth,
Fever - I'm afire
Fever, yea I burn forsooth.

Verse 4:
Captain Smith and Pocahantas
Had a very mad affair,
When her daddy tried to kill him, she said,
"Daddy-o don't you dare."

CHORUS:
Give me fever, with his kisses,
Fever when he holds me tight.
Fever - I'm his Missus
Oh Daddy won't you treat him right.

Verse 5:
Now you've listened to my story
Here's the point that I have made:
Chicks were born to give you fever
Be it Farenheit or Centigrade.

CHORUS:
They give you fever when you kiss them,
Fever if you live and learn.
Fever - till you sizzle
What a lovely way to burn.